ORIGAMI

30 stunning & original paper creations

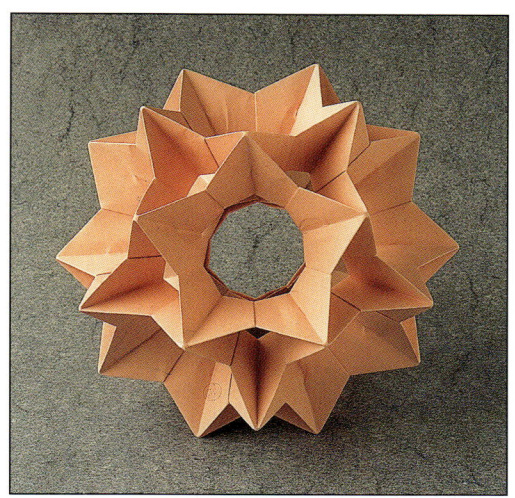

PAUL JACKSON

BARNES
& NOBLE
BOOKS

NEW YORK

This edition published by Barnes & Noble, Inc.,
by arrangement with Anness Publishing Limited

2003 Barnes & Noble Books

M 10 9 8 7 6 5 4 3 2

ISBN 0-7607-4181-6

© Anness Publishing Limited 1996, 2003

Publisher: Joanna Lorenz
Project Editor: Fiona Eaton
Designer: Lilian Lindblom
Contributors: Paul Jackson, Angela A'Court
Photographer: Martin Norris
Jacket Photographer: Amanda Heywood
Illustrator: Lorraine Harrison

Printed and bound in China

CONTENTS

INTRODUCTION

It is not difficult to understand why origami is the most popular of all papercrafts: the art is very inexpensive, can be done anywhere at any time and requires no equipment or facilities other than a sheet of paper and a firm surface to work on.

This book has three sections, which divide the designs into *Simple Projects*, *Intermediate Projects* and *Advanced Projects* according to their level of difficulty. Do not to be too ambitious too soon.

The last section, *Origami Techniques*, introduces the basics. If you are new to origami refer to them before you start. Readers who have folded before will find these pages a useful refresher.

Although origami is defined as "the art of paper folding", most paper folders spend little time thinking about paper, preferring to get straight down to the business of folding, frequently with whatever paper happens to be to hand. Consideration for the choice of paper can significantly improve the look of what you make and increase your pleasure in folding it.

The easiest and cheapest source of good quality practice paper is photocopy (Xerox) paper.

For two-tone models, origami paper bought in packets is ideal. However, it can be difficult to find and is relatively expensive.

Patterned gift-wrap paper is a good alternative. It is also worth starting a collection of unusual papers. A huge range can be found in art, craft and graphic supplies shops. And why not experiment with old posters and with all sorts of paper?

In many ways, nothing could be more basic than folding a sheet of paper. Yet, despite this wonderful simplicity, there are a few guidelines to follow that will make the process of folding easier and very satisfying. Please follow them:
• Check that the paper you are folding is exactly square.
• Do not fold against a soft surface, such as a carpet, your lap or bedsheets. Fold against a hard surface such as a large hardback book or a table.
• Crease slowly, firmly and accurately. Form the early creases with particular care – if they are incorrectly placed all the later, smaller creases will be difficult to place accurately and will look messy.
• The instructions and symbols on one step will create a shape which looks like the next step but stripped of its symbols. So, you must always look ahead to the next step to see what shape you are trying to make. Never look at steps in isolation, but see them as being interconnected, like links in a chain.

GLIDER

*This design is one of a number of similar gliders of Chinese origin,
all of which fly extremely well.*

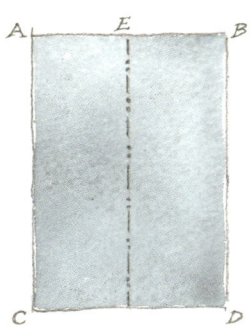

1 Fold the sheet in half down the middle, as a mountain fold. Unfold.

2 Fold in corners A & B to the centre crease.

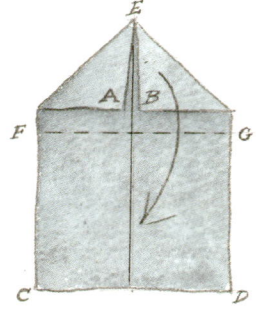

3 Fold down E along crease FG. Note that FG is a little below the level of AB.

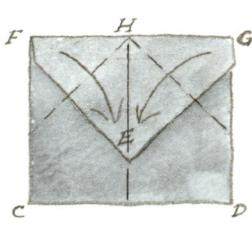

4 Fold in corners F & G, leaving E exposed.

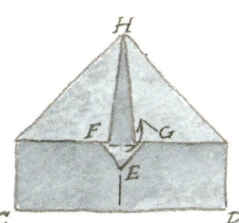

5 Fold up E over F & G.

6 Mountain fold D to C.

7 Before creasing, press flat the existing creases. Then, make the wing creases from the nose tip at H. To fly the glider, hold as shown at the point of balance, and release smoothly but firmly.

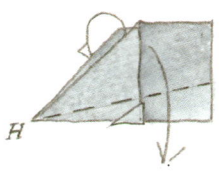

CANDY BAG

*If folded from greaseproof paper, this practical design will hold fries
and other oily or sticky foods. For extra strength, fold two squares
together. For sweets or candies, use any paper, not too thin.*

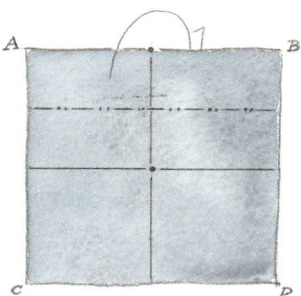

1 Fold and unfold
the paper in half
horizontally and vertically.
Mountain fold edge AB to
the centre crease.

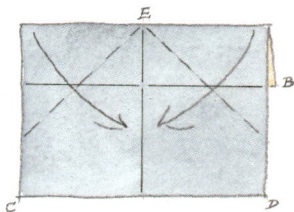

2 Fold in the top corners
to the centre crease.

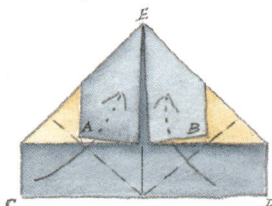

3 Similarly, fold in
bottom corners
C & D, but tucking them
beneath A & B, to lock
them flat.

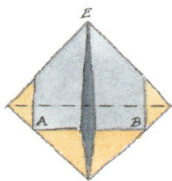

4 Valley fold in half
across the middle,
then . . .

5 . . . mountain fold
in half, to create a
flexible crease. Open out
the bag.

6 The Candy Bag
complete.

Butterfly

There are a great many origami butterflies in all manner of styles, some very complex. This is one of the simplest. It is important to use origami paper, so that white triangles appear at the edges between the coloured wings, to separate them visually. Cut a square of origami paper in half to create a 2 x 1 rectangle. Start coloured side up.

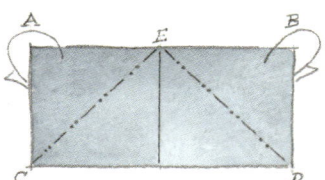

1 Fold corners A & B behind to the centre.

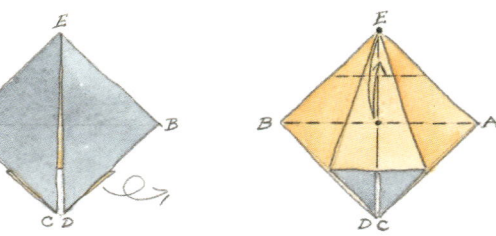

2 Fold EC & ED to the centre crease, allowing corners A & B to flip outwards . . .

3 . . . like this. Compare the position of the lettered corners with their position in Step 2. Turn over.

4 First, crease from B to A, across the middle. Then, fold E to the centre point.

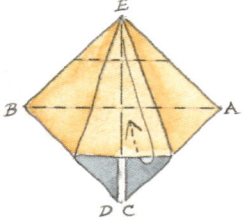

5 Re-form the Step 4 creases, but this time tuck E up under the horizontal edge.

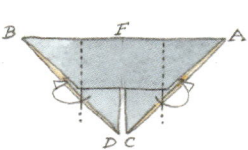

6 With vertical creases that run inside up to edge BA, mountain fold the loose corners behind as far as they will go.

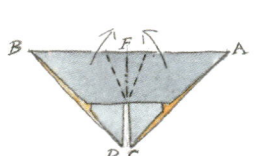

7 Make a mountain and two valley creases where shown, to create the body and to swivel points D & C apart.

8 The Butterfly complete.

SAMPAN

*This is a simplified version of a sampan with a canopy over each end of the boat.
Both designs feature an extraordinary move – here shown in Steps 7–9 – in which
the entire shape is turned inside out. With a little extra folding, one end of the
sampan can be blunted to create a rowing boat. Use a square of paper.
If using origami paper, start coloured side up.*

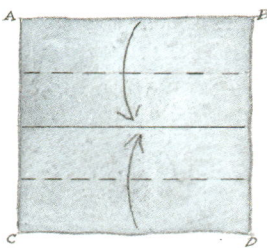

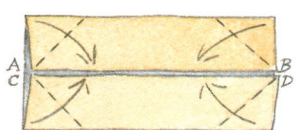

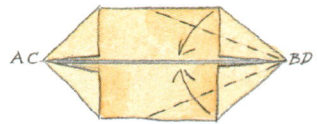

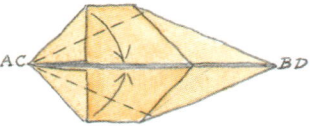

1 Crease and unfold across the centre. Fold the top and bottom edges to the crease.

2 Fold in the corners.

3 Narrow the corner at the right, as though making the familiar paper dart.

4 Repeat at the left, overlapping the Step 4 creases.

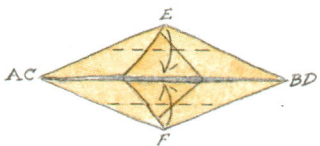

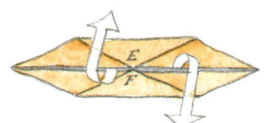

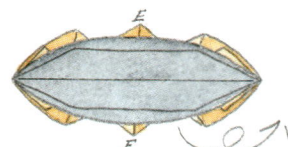

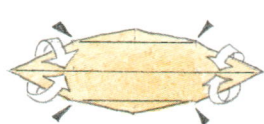

5 Fold in E & F to the centre crease. The paper is thick, so press firmly.

6 Open out all the layers revealing the coloured base . . .

7 . . . like this, to form a loose boat shape. Turn over.

8 To lock the sampan, push down on the four arrowed corners, so that the whole of the structure inverts and turns inside out!

9 The Sampan complete.

DUCK STEP

Napkin folds always create a point of interest on a dining table.
The Duck Step is a basic form from which other varieties
of napkin fold can be made.

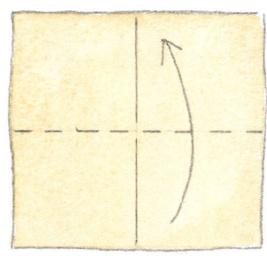

1 Completely unfold
a napkin, then fold the
bottom edge up to the top.

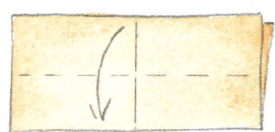

2 Fold the top edge
down to the crease.

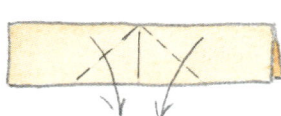

3 Fold each half of the
top edge down the
centre crease . . .

4 . . . like this. Turn the
napkin over.

5 Mountain fold the
right side behind
the left.

6 Valley fold the front
square up over the
triangle. Repeat behind.

7 The Duck Step napkin
complete.

CABLE BUFFET

The Cable Buffet server allows guests at a buffet or picnic to help themselves to food, a napkin and cutlery all at once.

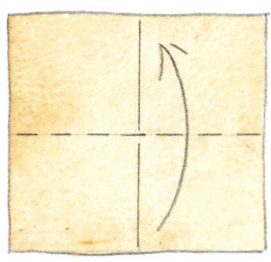

1 Completely unfold a napkin, then fold the bottom edge up to the top.

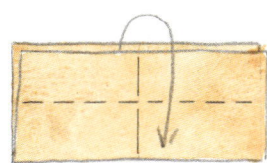

2 Fold the top layer down to the crease.

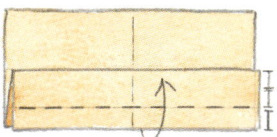

3 Fold the top layer back up a little way . . .

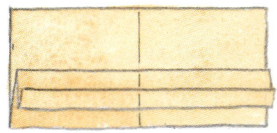

4 . . . like this. Turn the napkin over.

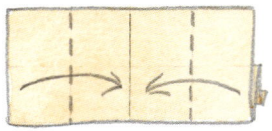

5 Fold the sides to the middle.

6 Tuck one half deep into the other, locking the napkin flat.

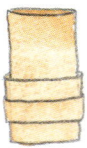

7 The Cable Buffet server complete. Insert cutlery into the pocket ready for the meal.

BISHOP

*The elegant curves and free-standing structure of this folded napkin create
a strong impact on any table.*

1 Completely unfold a
napkin, then fold the
bottom corner almost up
to the top.

2 Fold up the bottom
corners to the position
shown in Step 3.

3 Fold up the bottom
corner to the position
shown in Step 4.

4 Fold down the
front edge.

5 This is the basic shape.
The proportions are
important, so it may be
necessary to adjust some
of the folds. Turn the
napkin over.

6 Bend the left and right
halves forward.
Interlock one half into the
other to make a tube that
will not spring open.

7 The Bishop napkin
complete.

FISH

*This fish is pre-creased and collapsed into shape. When pre-creasing,
it is important to fold accurately (here, up to Step 5), otherwise the creases
will not fall into place to achieve Step 6. For extra flatness, a speck of glue
inside the mouth will close the layers.*

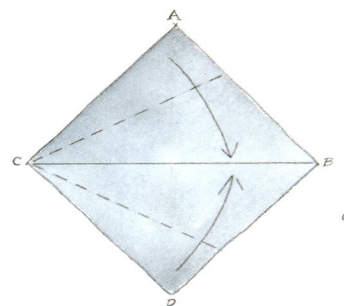

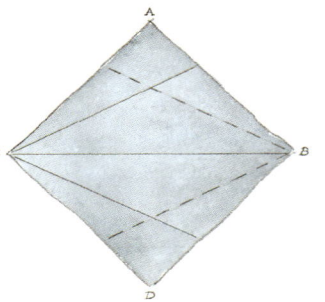

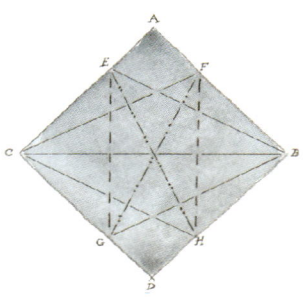

1 Crease and unfold the two diagonals, then bring edges CA & CD to the centre crease CB . . .

2 . . . like this. Unfold them.

3 Similarly, bring edges BA & BD to the centre crease. Unfold.

4 Connect the creases made in Steps 2–3 with mountain and valley creases, as shown. Be careful to place them accurately.

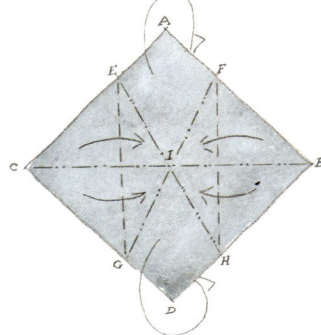

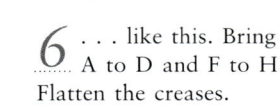

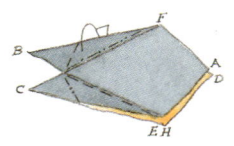

5 Collapse the paper along all the marked creases, noting which are mountains and which are valleys . . .

6 . . . like this. Bring A to D and F to H. Flatten the creases.

7 Lock by pleating one half of the tail fin into the body with a mountain fold and the other with a valley.

8 The Fish complete. Suspend it from a thread attached just behind the top corner at the point of balance.

SLEEPY DOG

The design is simple to make, but it is important to place C accurately in Steps 1 and 2. Once Step 3 has been achieved, the remaining folds fall naturally into place. Note the way in which the eyes are suggested. Use a square of origami paper, coloured side up.

1 Crease and unfold the two diagonals, then fold in corner C to the point described in Step 2.

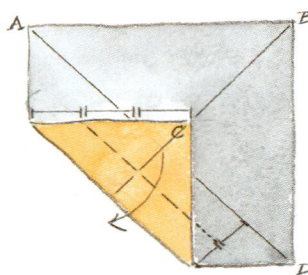

2 Note the position of C. Fold C back out, adding an extra crease as marked.

3 Mountain fold B behind, along the AD diagonal.

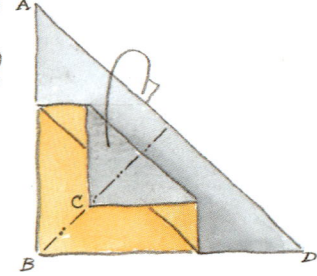

4 Mountain fold A behind to touch D.

5 Fold back points D & A to the outside.

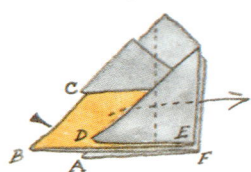

6 With a reverse fold, swing B through the middle. Note the position of the crease.

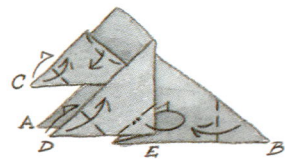

7 Mountain fold E behind. Repeat at F behind. Turn D, A & C inside out. Fold B forward. Curve the edge at the eye. Repeat for other eye.

8 The Sleepy Dog complete.

MODULAR DECORATION I

*A modular design is one in which a number of identical units are folded,
then locked together without glue to create a geometric form.*

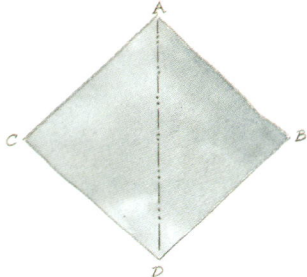

1 With a small square,
mountain fold down
the diagonal

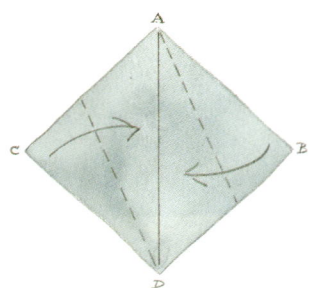

2 Fold in edges AB &
CD to the crease

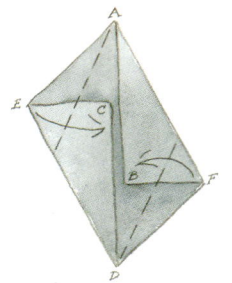

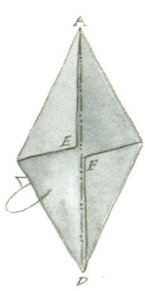

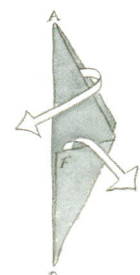

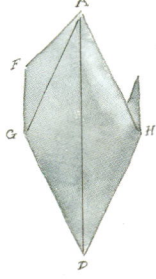

3 Fold in short edges AE & DF to the centre.

4 Mountain fold from A to D.

5 Unfold a little.

6 The module complete. Make four: two of one colour and two of another.

ASSEMBLY

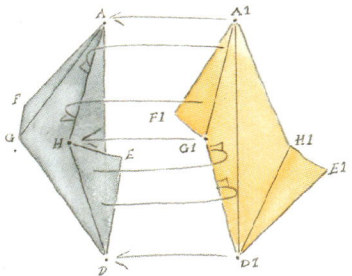

1 Edge A1, F1 on the right-hand module is tucked behind edge AH on the left-hand module. At the same time, edge DE on the left-hand module is tucked behind edge D1, G1 on the right-hand module. Note that A1 touches A, G1 touches H and D1 touches D.

2 This is the result. The lock is not strong, but when two other modules are locked in, so that the fourth locks into the first to close the circle, the complete structure will lock well.

3 The Modular Decoration complete. Suspend the finished module from a thread.

COLOUR CHANGE BIRD

The simple shape of the completed bird and the effectiveness of the colour
contrasts are achieved by a fluent and concise sequence of folds. Perhaps
it is too stylized for some people, but less can sometimes be more.
Use a square of origami paper, white side up.

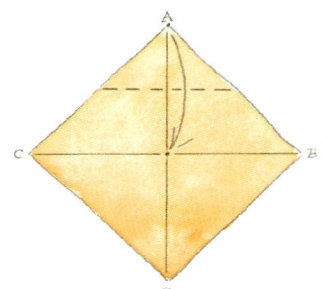

1 Crease and unfold the two diagonals, then fold corner A to the centre point.

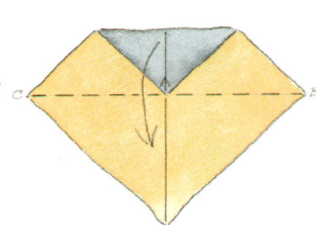

2 Roll the triangle downwards, along crease CB.

3 Fold C & B dot to dot, as shown.

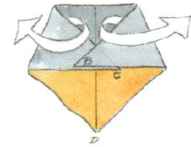

4 Unfold C & B.

5 Turn over.

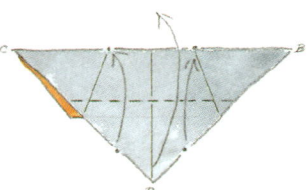

6 Fold dot to dot, aligning edges DC & DB with the tops of the creases made in Step 3.

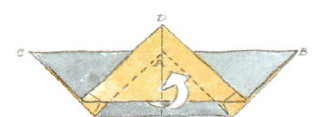

7 Pull out corner A.

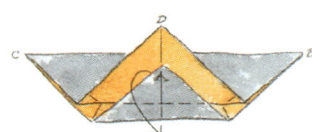

8 Fold down A, level with the folded edge.

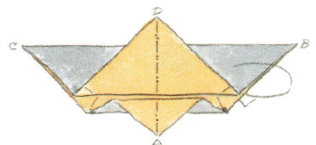

9 Fold B behind.

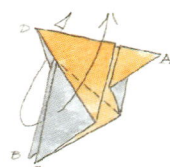

10 Fold up B & C along existing internal (hidden) creases made in Step 3.

11 Reverse fold D to create the head. Fold out the feet to create a stable base for the bird.

12 The Colour Change Bird complete.

MODULAR DECORATION II

The basic modules are very simple to make, but some thought must be given to assembling them correctly. Once locked, they will hold together very well.

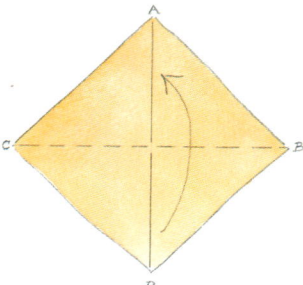

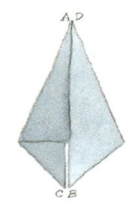

1 Crease and fold a vertical diagonal, then fold D up to A.

2 Fold edge AD,B forward to the vertical crease (valley fold) and edge AD,C behind to that crease (mountain fold).

3 This is the completed module. Make another.

ASSEMBLY

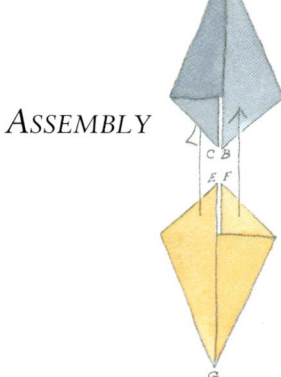

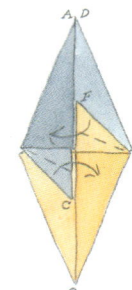

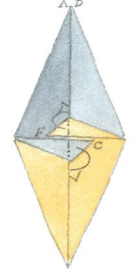

1 Take careful note of the lettered corners. Bring the two modules together, so that F is on top of B, and C is on top of E . . .

2 . . . like this. Fold F across to the horizontal. Repeat with C, then with E & B behind.

3 Lock the modules together by tucking F & C behind the vertical edges. Repeat behind with E & B.

4 Separate the modules by twisting one away from the other, so that they lie perpendicular to each other. Suspend the completed module from a thread.

HOUSE

Here is a remarkable sequence of three multiform designs which are all made from the same basic shape, the House. The designs shown here are not the full set: it is also possible to fold a dustpan, purse, fox puppet, crown . . . and very probably many others! Experiment by folding the paper this way and that to see what you can discover. Use a square of origami paper, white side up.

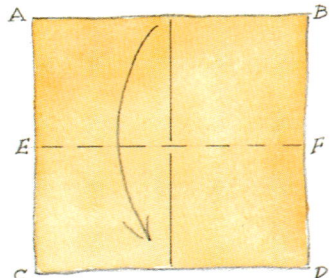

1 Crease and unfold down the middle of a square, then fold AB down to CD.

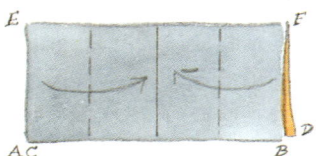

2 Fold the edges to the centre.

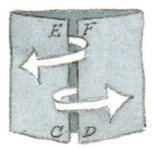

3 Unfold.

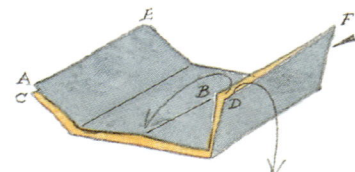

4 Lift up the edge BD,F. Separate B from D, applying pressure on the edges below F . . .

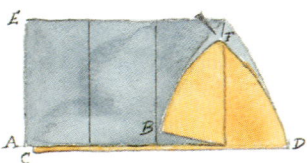

5 . . . like this. Pull B & D right apart and squash F flat.

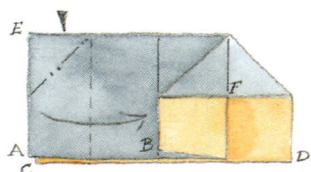

6 Repeat Steps 4–5 on the left, separating A from C and squashing E flat. Let A touch B.

7 The House complete. Children like to draw windows and a door to finish the design.

✳

3D HOUSE

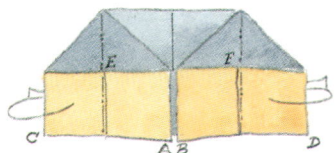

1 Complete Steps 1–6 of the House (see pages 26–7). Fold C & D behind.

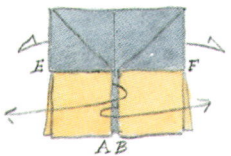

2 Unfold AC & BD.

3 The 3D House complete.

G. I. Cap

To make a full-size cap, use a square trimmed from a large format newspaper.

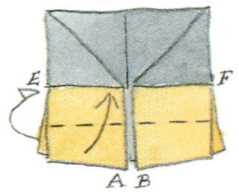

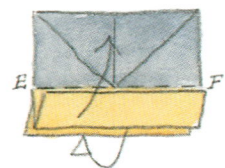

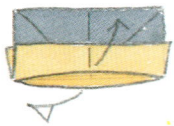

1 Begin with Step 2 of the 3D House (see page 28). Fold AB up to EF. Repeat behind.

2 Fold up the bottom section along crease EF. Repeat behind.

3 Open out the cap.

4 The G.I. Cap complete.

STAR

The shape made in Step 7 is known in origami as the Preliminary Base,
so called because other, more advanced bases can be developed from it,
including the Bird and Frog bases. Use a square of paper or perhaps
paper-backed foil, coloured side up.

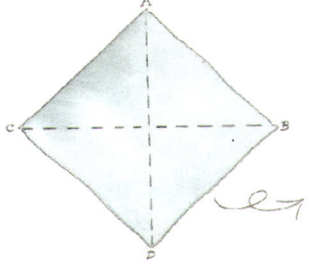

1 Crease and unfold both diagonals as valleys. Turn over.

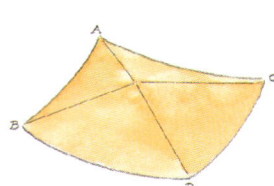

2 Check that the diagonals are now mountain creases.

3 Fold and unfold in half down the middle, then . . .

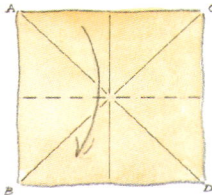

4 . . . fold in half across the middle.

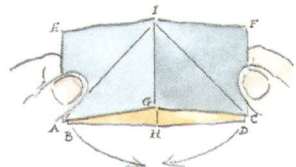

5 Hold as shown. If the mountain and valley creases have been placed correctly, a 3D diamond shape will emerge when the hands are swung towards each other . . .

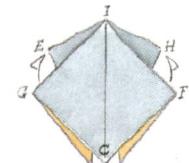

6 . . . like this. Flatten G against E and F against H.

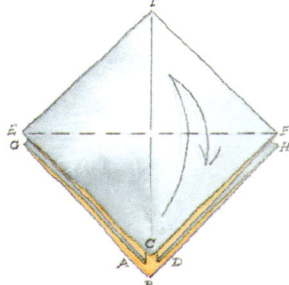

7 Fold the single layer corner C up to I, then unfold.

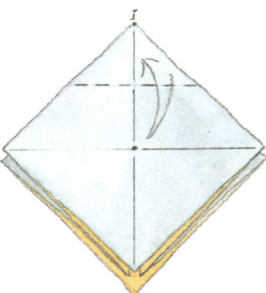

8 Fold I down to the centre point. Unfold. Open the paper a little.

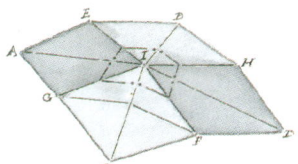

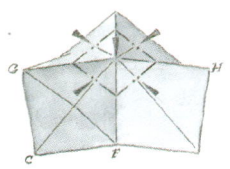

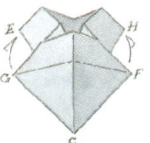

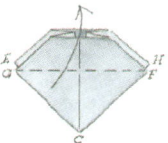

9 The crease formed in Step 8 makes a square. Crease the four sides of the square as mountains . . .

10 . . . like this. Flatten the centre square, then push it downwards into the paper . . .

11 . . . like this. Re-form the Step 8 shape, but with I now sunk inside the paper.

12 Fold up C again.

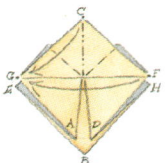

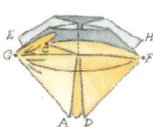

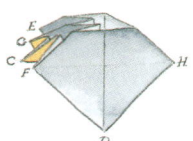

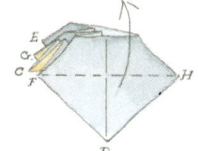

13 Swing C down to corner G, whilst also bringing corner F across to touch G. The crease from G is a mountain.

14 Halfway.

15 Complete. Note how F, C, G & E lie one behind the other.

16 Similarly, fold up D along line FH . . .

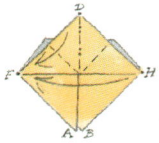

17 . . . swing towards corner F, bringing H across to touch corner F. Repeat this sequence with A then B, turning the paper over and around each time. Fan out the points in a symmetrical pattern.

WATERBOMB

Many people – particularly mischievous children – have learnt how to make a waterbomb, but without practice it is very easy to forget how to lock it. Without a good lock, it cannot contain the water it is designed to hold!

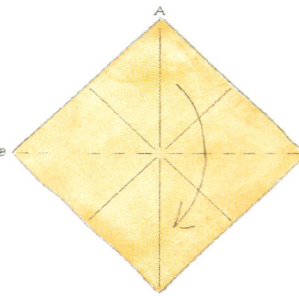

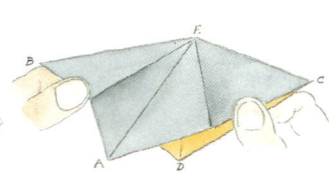

1 Mountain fold horizontally and vertically across the paper. Unfold each time.

2 Form a vertical valley diagonal (the other creases are mountains). Unfold.

3 Fold A down to D.

4 Hold as shown. If the mountains and valleys have been placed correctly, the paper will form a 3D pyramid when the hands are swung towards each other . . .

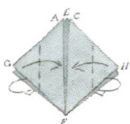

5 . . . like this. Flatten A against B, and D against C.

6 Fold A & C up to E. Repeat behind with B & D. (Note: to increase the size of the hole through which air is blown to inflate the Waterbomb, fold the corners short of E. A hole that is too small is difficult to blow through.)

7 Fold G & H to the centre. Repeat behind.

8 Fold A & C into the centre at G & H.

9 Valley fold the small triangle above A into the pocket made by separating the layers above G. Repeat with C on the right and twice more behind with B and D.

10 The Waterbomb is now locked, front and back. Blow into the hole at the bottom to make it 3D. If the hole is too small, enlarge it.

11 The Waterbomb complete.

TRADITIONAL BOX

This is perhaps the classic origami box. It is quick and simple to make,
and locks strongly. A box made from a slightly larger square will form a lid.
In Step 3, if the creases are not placed at the quarter points, but elsewhere,
taller or squatter boxes can be made. Use a square of strong paper.
If using origami paper, start white side up.

1 Mountain fold horizontally and vertically across the centre, unfolding each time.

2 Fold the corners to the centre. (The existing creases are mountains.)

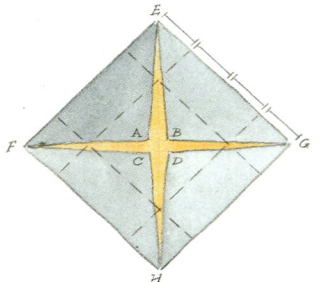

3 Fold each edge in turn to the centre point, unfolding each crease before making the next.

4 Pull open corners A & D.

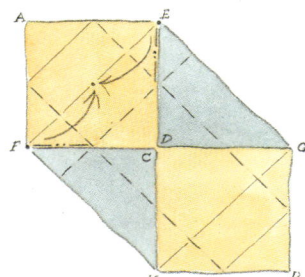

5 Re-crease valleys where shown.

6 Make the paper 3D by bringing F & E to the centre dot . . .

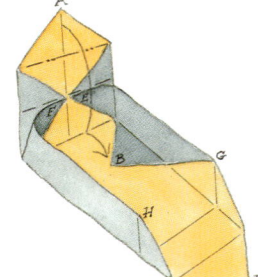

7 . . . like this. Lock the end of the box by folding A over the top and into the middle.

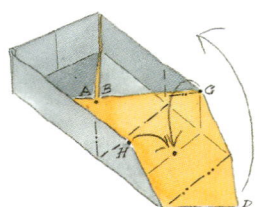

8 Repeat Steps 6–7 with H & G, folding D over the top to lock.

NESTING BIRD

The design features a peculiar and little-used manoeuvre at Steps 4–5, when one spike is pulled out from inside another that envelops it. The move is very satisfying! Begin with a square of paper, same colour both sides.

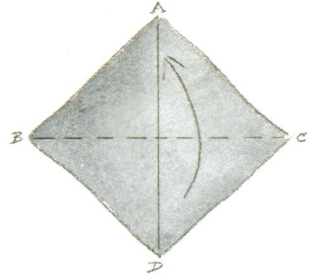

1 Crease and unfold a vertical diagonal, then fold D up to A.

2 Fold edges AD,B and AD,C to the centre crease.

3 Fold out corners B & C.

4 Note the shape of the paper. Pull out D from inside A . . .

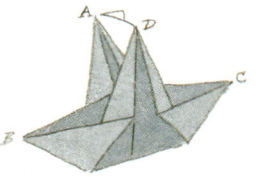

5 . . . like this. Flatten D on top of A.

6 Turn over.

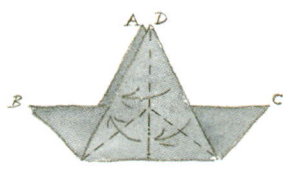

7 Collapse the paper as shown, separating A from D and bringing C to touch B.

8 Lift up corner C, squashing the paper flat at the left.

9 Fold B behind.

10 Reverse fold D. Fold out the bottom corners to stay away from the wings and so create a stable base for the bird to balance on.

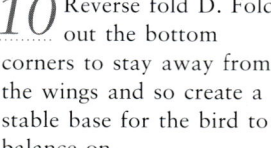

BEAK

This is a variation on a well-known origami "action" theme.
The mechanism will be familiar to knowledgeable paper folders, but here
the eyes are made differently. It is important to use origami paper,
to achieve a contrast of colour for the eyes and the inside of the mouth.

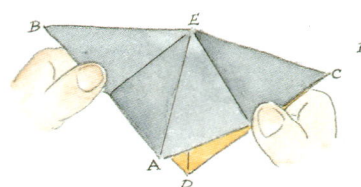

1 Begin with Step 4 of the Waterbomb project (see pages 32–3). Flatten the paper. The colour should be on the outside.

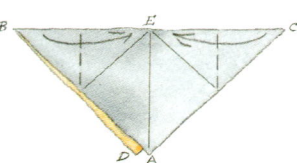

2 Fold B & C to E.

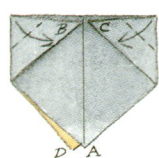

3 Fold in the corners.

4 (The instructions now refer to B only, but repeat all Steps with C.) Swivel B behind and downwards . . .

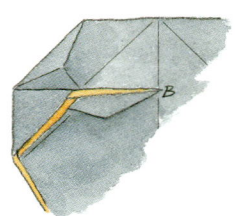

5 . . . like this . . .

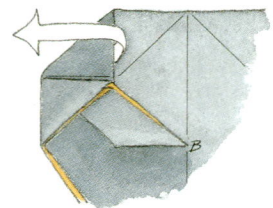

6 . . . and flatten. Unfold.

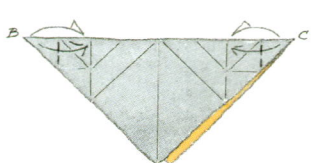

7 Fold B & C inwards, unfolding the paper to an open square to do this, . . .

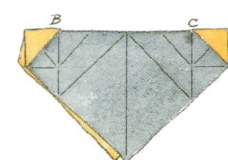

8 . . . like this. Re-crease back to Step 6 following Steps 2–6.

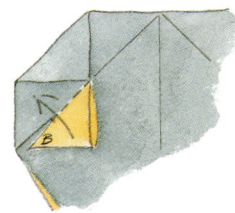

9 Note the new shape at B. Fold up triangle B.

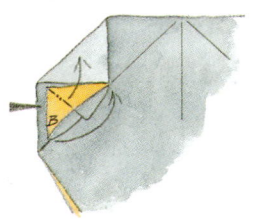

10 Open and squash flat the triangle, forming a square.

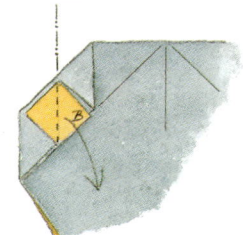

11 Swivel the square down and to the right along a hidden crease.

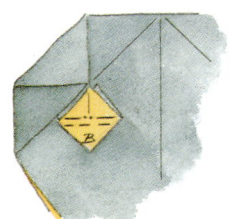

12 Pleat the eye.

13 The Beak complete. Hold as shown and move your hands to and fro to make the mouth open and close!

LIGHTHEARTED

In this design, the final shape is unimpressive, but reveals a translucent heart when held against the light! Use a square of thin paper; thicker papers will not reveal the heart.

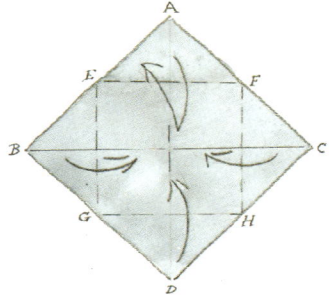

1 Crease and unfold the horizontal diagonal BC. Fold the four corners to the centre.

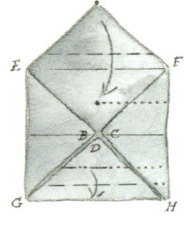

2 Fold down corner A as shown. Pleat triangle DGH as shown.

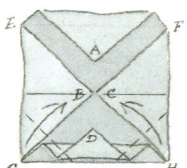

3 Fold in corners G & H. Note the very small intrusion of the crease into the D triangle. This is important, as it affects the proportion of the heart.

4 Unfold Step 3.

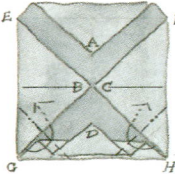

5 Re-crease Step 3, but reverse folding the top part of each crease to push G under B, and H under C.

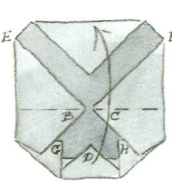

6 Fold in half.

7 Fold in E & F just a little way.

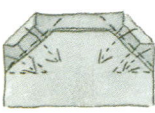

8 Fold over as shown, locking the edges into the pockets made in Step 5.

9 Fold the excess paper into the top pocket.

10 Note that the shape is locked flat.

11 To see the heart, hold the paper up to a window or other diffuse light source (but not the sun).

STAR BOX

It is relatively easy to make a square, straight-sided box, such as the Traditional Box project, but the technical complexities increase as the final shape becomes less plain. This design is pleasingly bold. Use a square of origami paper, with the coloured side outwards.

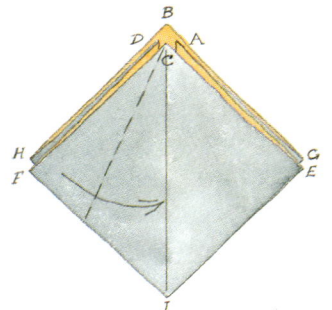

1 Begin with Step 7 of the Star (see pages 30–31), turned upside down. Fold FC to centre.

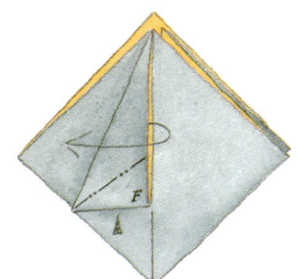

2 Lift up the single top layer and squash F . . .

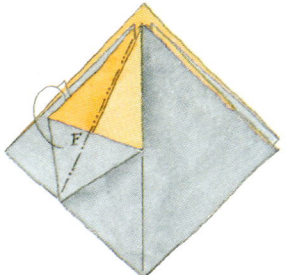

3 . . . like this. Fold the outer section of the squash behind.

4 Repeat Steps 2–3 with E.

5 Turn over.

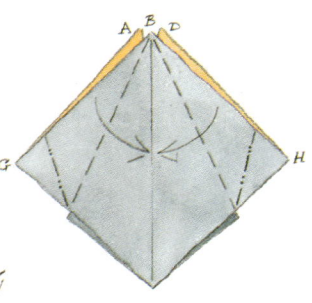

6 Repeat Steps 2–4 with G & H.

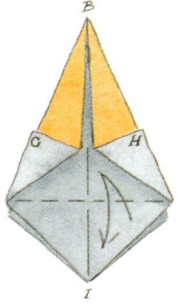

7 Crease and unfold across the full width of the paper. To help Step 9, the valley can be further creased as a mountain.

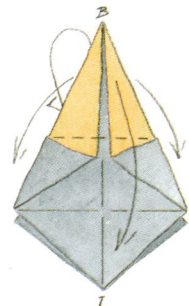

8 Fold down B as far as it will go. Repeat with A,C & D.

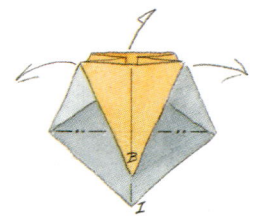

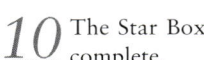

9 Open out the box, flattening the bottom along the Step 7 creases.

10 The Star Box complete.

JUMPING FROG

There are many origami jumping frogs, most – like this one – made by creating
a frog shape, then pleating across the body to create the spring. This version is
a particularly athletic jumper. Use a square of green coloured paper.

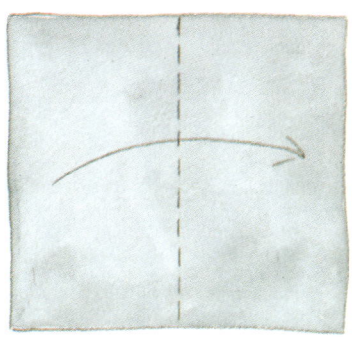

1 Fold a square in half down the middle.

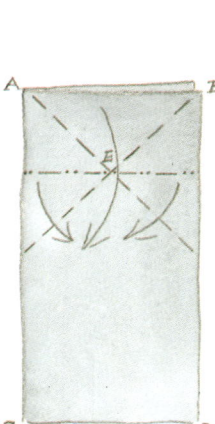

2 The paper is now two layers thick, but will be referred to as though it is a single layer. Collapse AB to make the shape seen in Step 6 of the Waterbomb project (see pages 32–33).

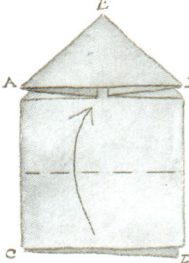

3 Fold up edge CD to AB.

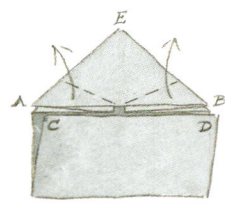

4 Swing out A & B. Note that they do not touch E, but protrude to the side.

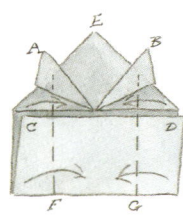

5 Fold in the sides.

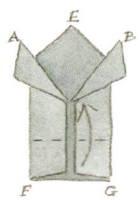

6 Fold edge FG to the centre point.

7 Fold down corners F & G . . .

8 . . . like this.

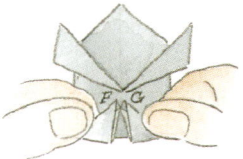

9 Hold tightly as shown. Slide F & G away from H . . .

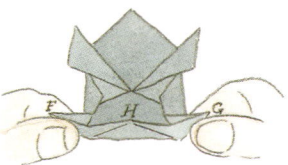

10 . . . like this, keeping firm hold of F & G. When F & G have been pulled out as far to the side as they will go, flatten the paper . . .

11 . . . like this. Fold down F & G.

12 Turn over.

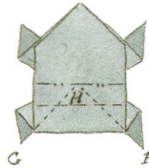

13 Make a pleat, with the mountain crease passing through H. The paper is very thick, so apply considerable pressure. But the frog will jump further if the creases are not put in too firmly.

14 The Jumping Frog complete.

15 To make it jump, put your finger on its back. Flatten the pleat and slide your finger off! With practice, it will jump quite a distance.

BIRD

*This design is straightforward until Step 9, when the difficult 3D crimp
transforms an ordinary flat bird into a 3D bird with a pleasingly rounded shape.
Use a square piece of paper, coloured the same on both sides.*

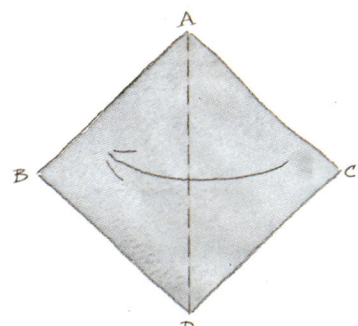

1 Fold C across to B.

2 Fold A down to D.

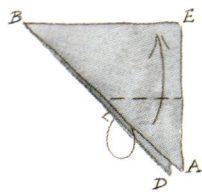

3 Fold A up to E.
Repeat behind.

4 Fold in the corners.

5 Unfold crease BC,E.

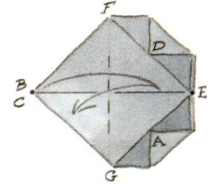

6 Fold BC to E, but
creasing halfway from
the existing centre crease
to corners F & G. Unfold,
then re-fold back to step 5.

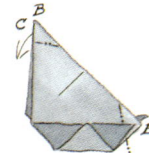

7 Reverse corners
BC & E.

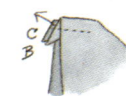

8 Reverse corner C only,
creating the open beak.

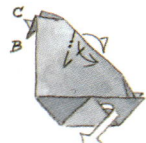

9 Pull down the triangles front and back as a base for
the bird. Crease a mountain fold front and back, so
that when folded over the valley made in Step 6, the bird
becomes rounded. Unfold the spine a little to assist with
this crimp. The bird has to be forced into shape, but will
lock strongly when in position. To make the rounded
shape push the paper outwards from the inside.

10 The Bird complete.

BUILDING

The design shows how the rectangles and triangles that are created naturally by folding a square along halves and quarters, can be articulated to create a form such as this semi-abstract building, complete with colour-change roofs. Use a square of origami paper, white side up.

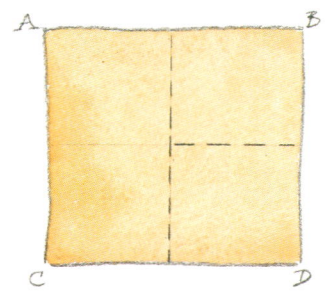

1 Crease as shown. Note the short crease at the right.

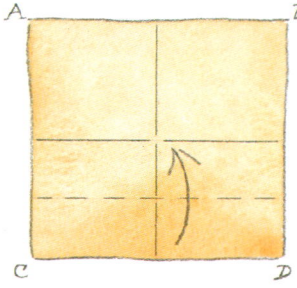

2 Fold edge CD up to the centre crease, then fold in half down the middle.

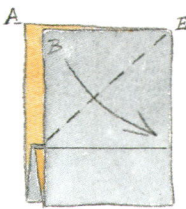

3 Fold down corner B.

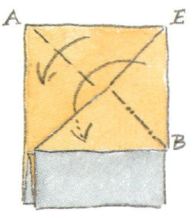

4 Reverse fold corner E behind B.

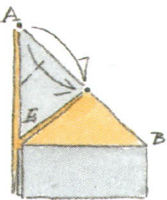

5 Fold corner A as shown, opening the paper to do this.

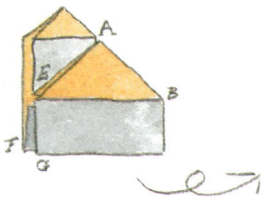

6 Turn over.

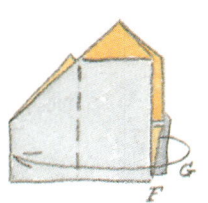

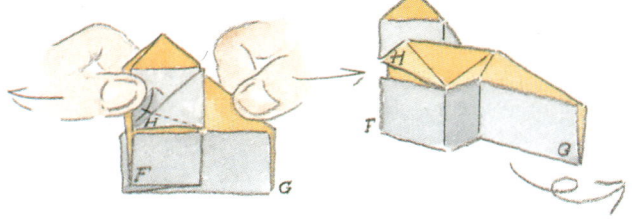

7 Swing F over to the left.

8 Hold as shown and move your hands apart. Corner H will lift. Crease and flatten H as shown . . .

9 . . . like this. Turn over.

10 The Building complete.

PIG

The Pig, although a fairly complex project, is rewarding to construct, especially when the finished animal emerges as the steps are completed.

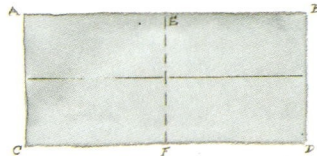

1 Crease and unfold the long horizontal centre crease, then crease and unfold the shorter axis.

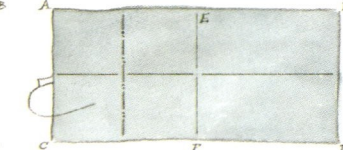

2 Fold edge AC behind.

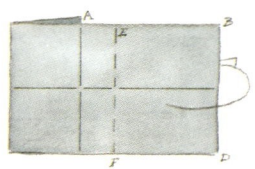

3 Fold edge BD behind to the crease made in Step 2.

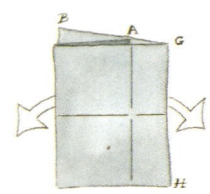

4 Unfold.

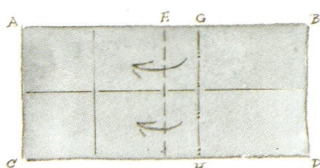

5 Pleat along existing creases EF & GH.

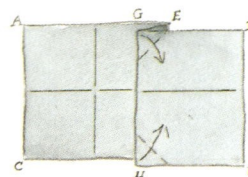

6 Turn in corners G & H.

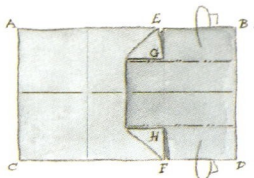

7 Swivel B & D behind, along horizontal mountain creases. Note the shape of Step 8.

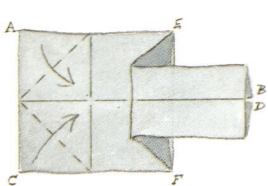

8 Fold in corners A & C.

9 Fold A & C back out, the creases tapering towards I.

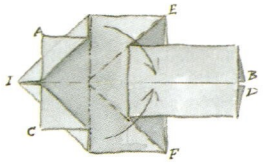

10 Collapse as shown, to make the paper 3D.

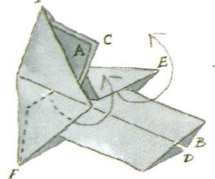

11 Pull out the hidden ledge . . .

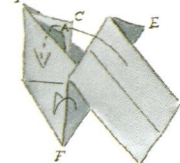

12 . . . and feed it back into the pig between A & C . . .

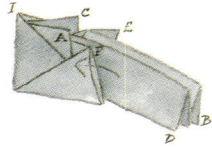

13 . . . like this, bringing F & E back together again.

14 The manoeuvre is complete – its purpose is to stop the pig from splaying its front legs. Turn the paper the right way up.

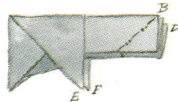

15 Reverse fold at B & D.

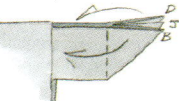

16 Fold B & D towards the neck.

17 Create two reverse folds near the snout, forming a crimp.

18 Fold the snout over and over. Fold the ears forward.

19 Crimp the neck, lowering the head.

20 Pleat the tail.

STANDING HEART

Hearts are a favourite origami theme. This conventional single heart could make an attractive standing ornament for a mantelpiece or desk top. Use a square of red/white origami paper, red side up.

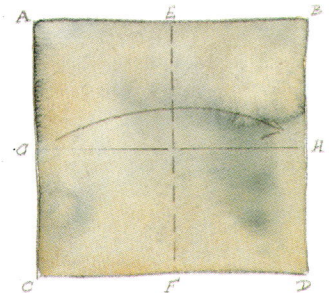

1 Crease and unfold across the middle, then fold AC across to BD.

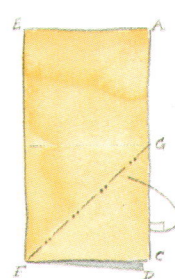

2 Mountain fold corners C & D inside.

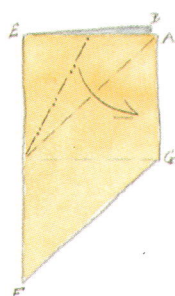

3 Squash fold corner E.

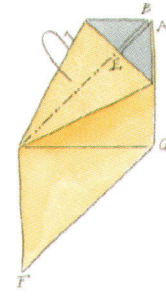

4 Fold the outer section of the squash fold behind.

5 Open the paper between G & H. Turn over to see . . .

6 . . . a pyramid. Corner I is the apex (the corner nearest to you). Push on I so that it inverts and the paper pops inside out. Corner I is now the furthest point from you, not the nearest.

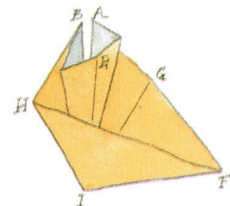

7 This is the shape. Note I.

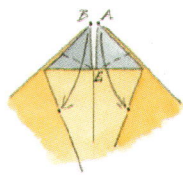

8 Fold down B & A, dot to dot.

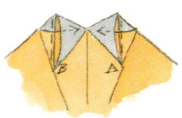

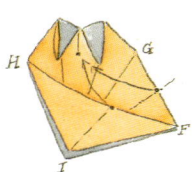

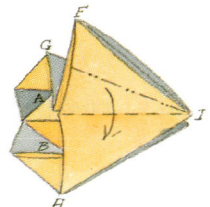

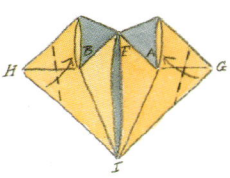

9 Tuck the excess paper into the pockets at B & A.

10 Collapse as shown, folding the two outer dots onto the inner one.

11 Squash F, presently standing upright.

12 Fold in H & G.

13 Fold over G to lock the triangle to the edge behind.

14 Open out the pocket between F & I . . .

15 . . . like this, flattening the paper.

16 Partly close the pocket again. Turn over.

17 The Standing Heart complete.

CHINESE VASE

This design has a beautifully direct sequence of folds, climaxed by the extraordinary opening out from 2D to 3D. Use a square of paper, not too small. If using origami paper, start white side up.

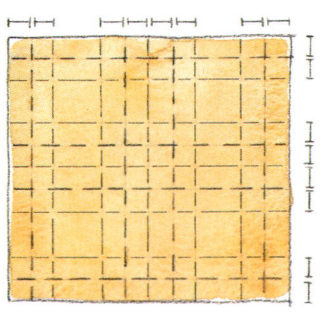

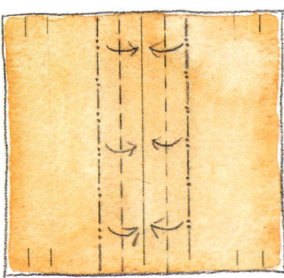

1 Crease a square into eight equal divisions, then carefully cut off two squares horizontally and vertically, to create a 6 x 6 grid.

2 Add extra creases where shown.

3 Pleat the paper as shown.

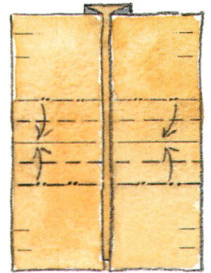

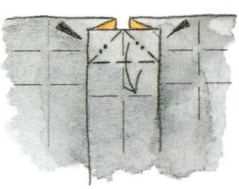

4 Similarly, pleat horizontally.

5 This is the shape of the paper. Turn over.

6 This is the shape.

7 Lift and squash the end of each pleat . . .

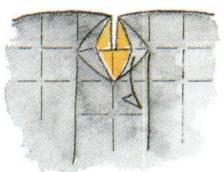

8 . . . like this.

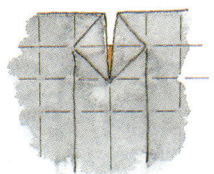

9 Repeat along each edge.

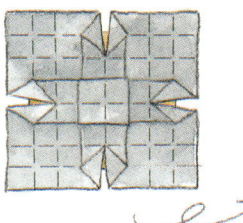

10 Here are the squashed pleats. Turn over.

11 Crease and unfold each loose corner at the pleats. This is to prepare for Step 14.

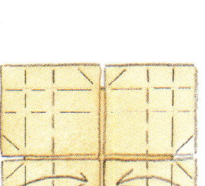

12 Fold the sides to the middle.

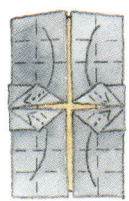

13 Fold the top and bottom edges to the middle, tucking the corners deep into the pockets.

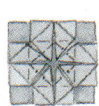

14 Fold the loose corners inside, to create a square opening . . .

15 . . . like this. Turn over.

16 This is the fun part! Carefully tease out the trapped layers inside the pleats to make the vase 3D. Do this by rotating the paper frequently, so that all four sides are developed equally.

17 This is the result. Put a finger into the vase and round out the square, flat corners at the top.

ELECTRA

An appeal of modular folding is that spectacular structures can be made from simple units, so that the whole is very much more than the sum of its parts. Thirty modules are needed for this design. Fold them all carefully, then slot them together, with diligent regard for the "5 and 3" (pentagons and triangles) interlocking pattern. If using origami paper, start with the coloured side up.

1 Crease and unfold both diagonals as valleys. Turn over.

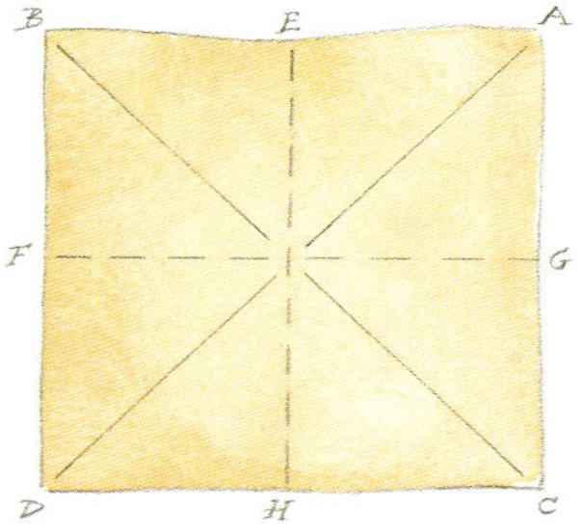

2 Crease and unfold horizontally and vertically. (The diagonals are mountains.)

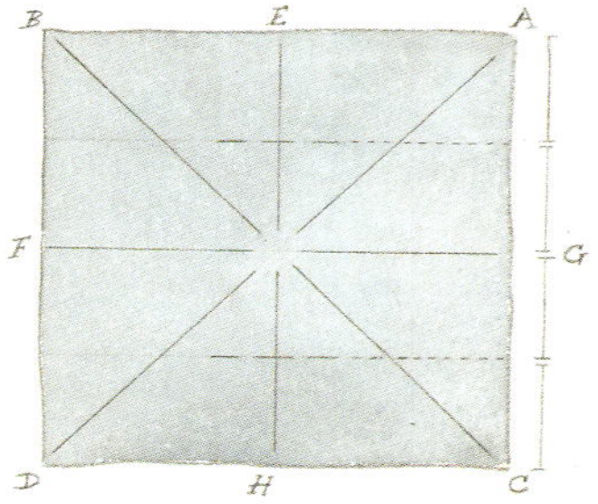

3 Pinch the quarter points along crease EH.

4 Fold corners B & C to the middle.

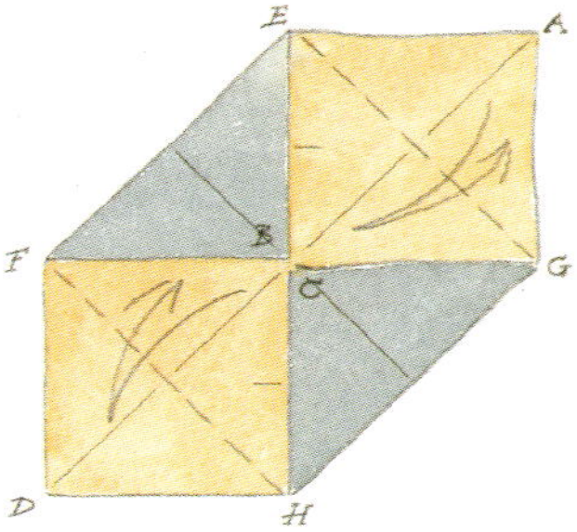

5 Fold and unfold corners A & D.

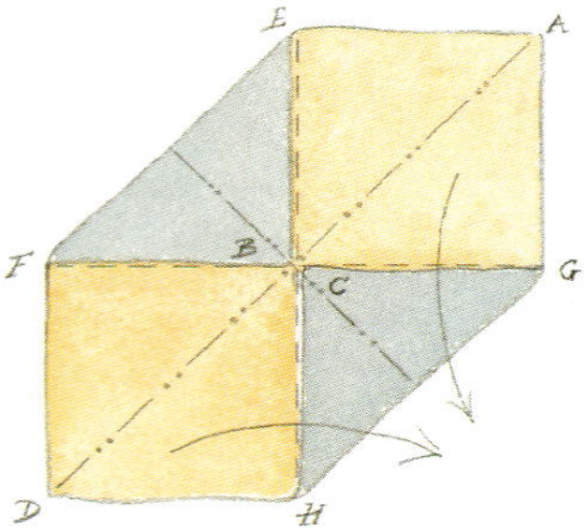

6 Collapse all the creases.

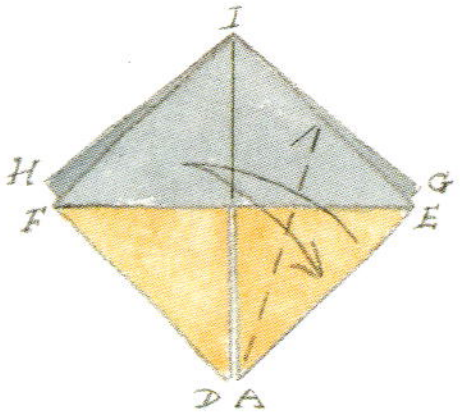

7 Form a crease between A and the pinch made in Step 3, folding E across to the left side. Unfold.

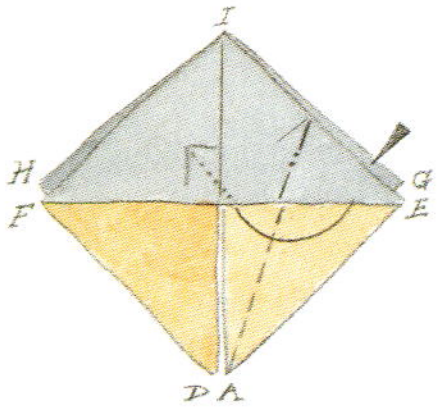

8 Re-form the crease, but reverse fold E inside.

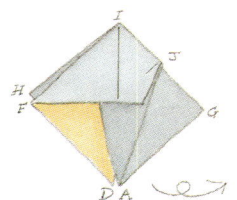

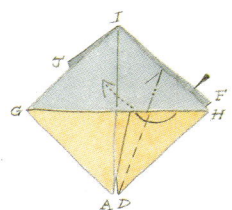

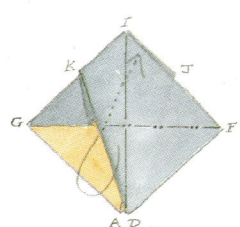

9 This is the result. Turn over.

10 Repeat Steps 7–9 with H.

11 Fold K across to the left, allowing the triangle above D to swivel inside and to the right. Repeat behind with J.

12 Mountain fold D inside, creating a pocket below K. Repeat with A.

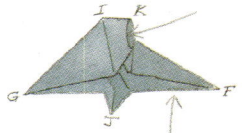

13 This is the completed module. Note the closed pockets below J & K and the extended flaps at F & G.

ASSEMBLY

1 Tuck the extended flap on one module (F1), deep inside the pocket of another. To lock them together, fold F or G (depending on which one flap F1 has been tucked into) towards G1.

2 Repeat with the nearside flaps and pockets.

3 Lock 5 modules together, leaving no excess flaps in the centre of the pentagon. A sixth module is shown at the bottom of the drawing connecting two neighbouring pentagon modules, thereby creating a triangle with no loose flaps in its centre. The completed Electra is thus a combination of pentagons and triangles. Interlock the remaining modules following this pattern.

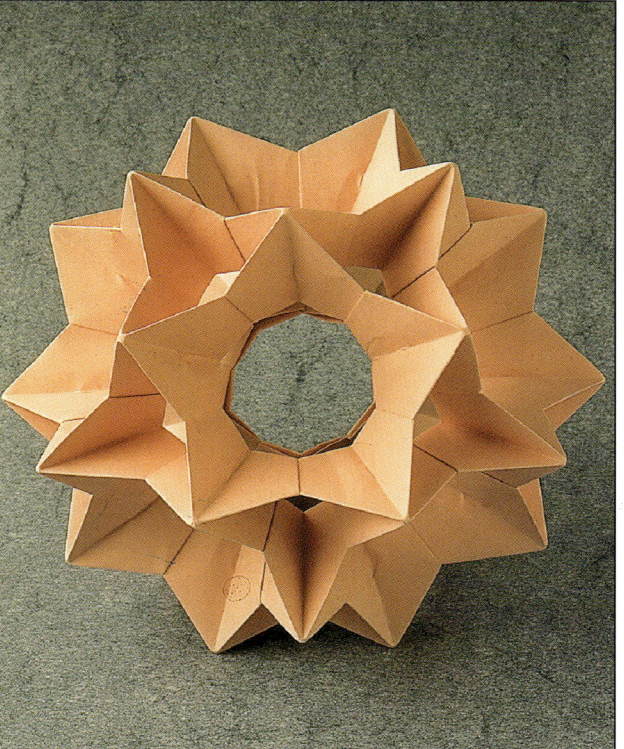

SEAL ON A ROCK

So called "double subjects" or "combination folds" are common in complex origami, where two subjects or objects are folded from a single sheet. Use a square of origami paper coloured side up or, for a better effect, two differently coloured or textured sheets folded back to back.

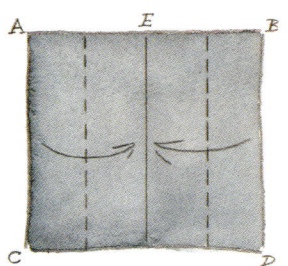

1 Crease and unfold down the centre, then fold the sides to the middle.

2 Reverse fold the top two corners.

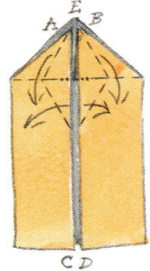

3 Collapse, folding A & B downwards and adding the reverse folds.

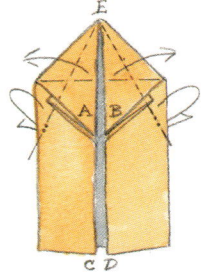

4 Fold as shown, allowing A & B to swivel outwards.

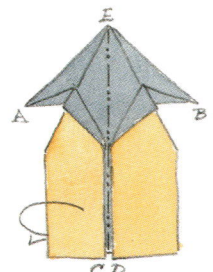

5 Mountain fold A behind.

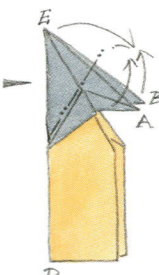

6 Reverse fold E, allowing A & B to pivot upwards to touch E.

7 Narrow the paper with two reverse folds.

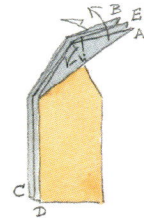

8 Pleat A & B.

9 Turn E inside out, lowering A & B.

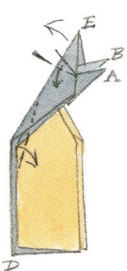

10 Crimp the neck upwards. Release paper for the tail. Repeat behind.

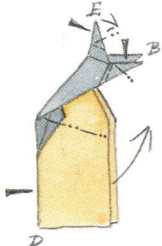

11 Crimp the head. Squash the flippers. Reverse fold the rock.

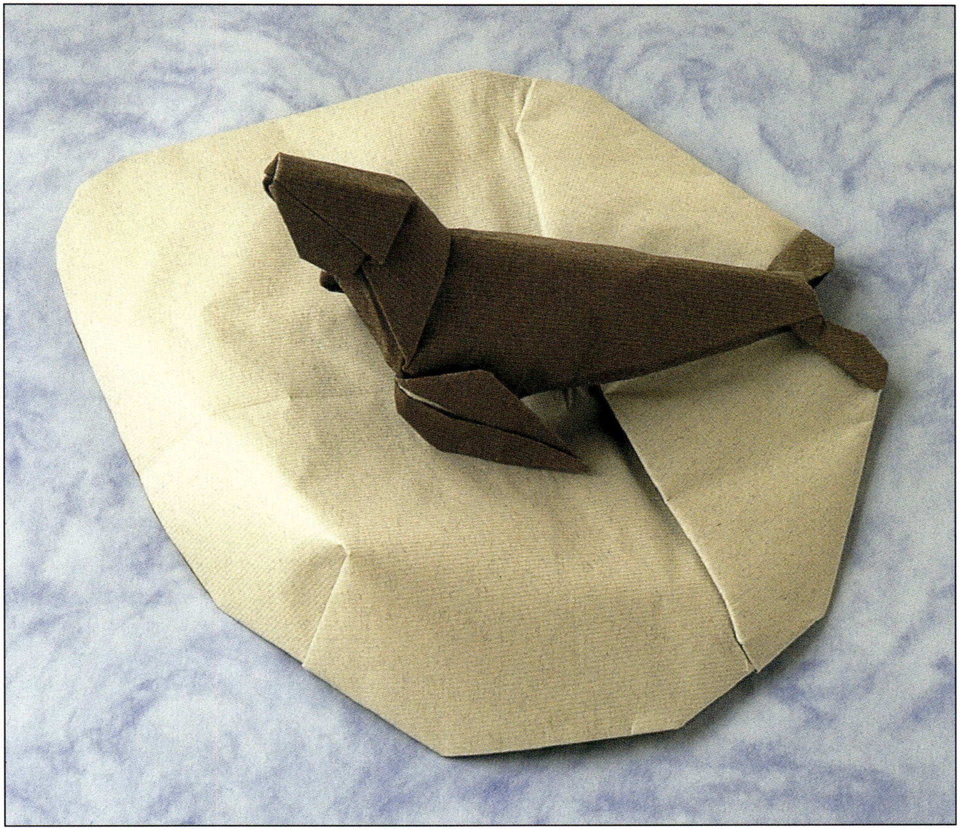

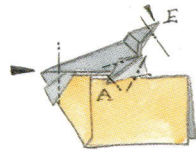

12 Reverse fold the snout. Round off the flippers. Sink the excess paper inside at the tail.

13 Crimp the rock to make it 3D.

14 The Seal on a Rock complete.

SYMBOLS

No sequence of origami diagrams can be followed without an understanding of the symbols they use. The meaning of most symbols is obvious and it is not necessary to learn them all, but it would be very helpful at least to learn the difference between the mountain and valley fold symbols. The other symbols can be learnt as they appear by referring back to this page.
The same symbols can be found in most origami books, whatever language they are written in, be it English, Spanish or even Japanese.
This standardization means that the language of origami is truly universal, and that enthusiasts can fold from almost any book, East or West.

valley

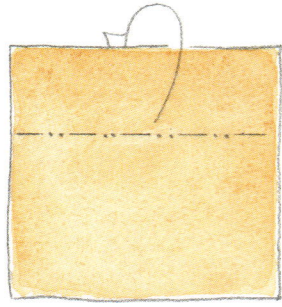 

mountain

turn over

existing creases

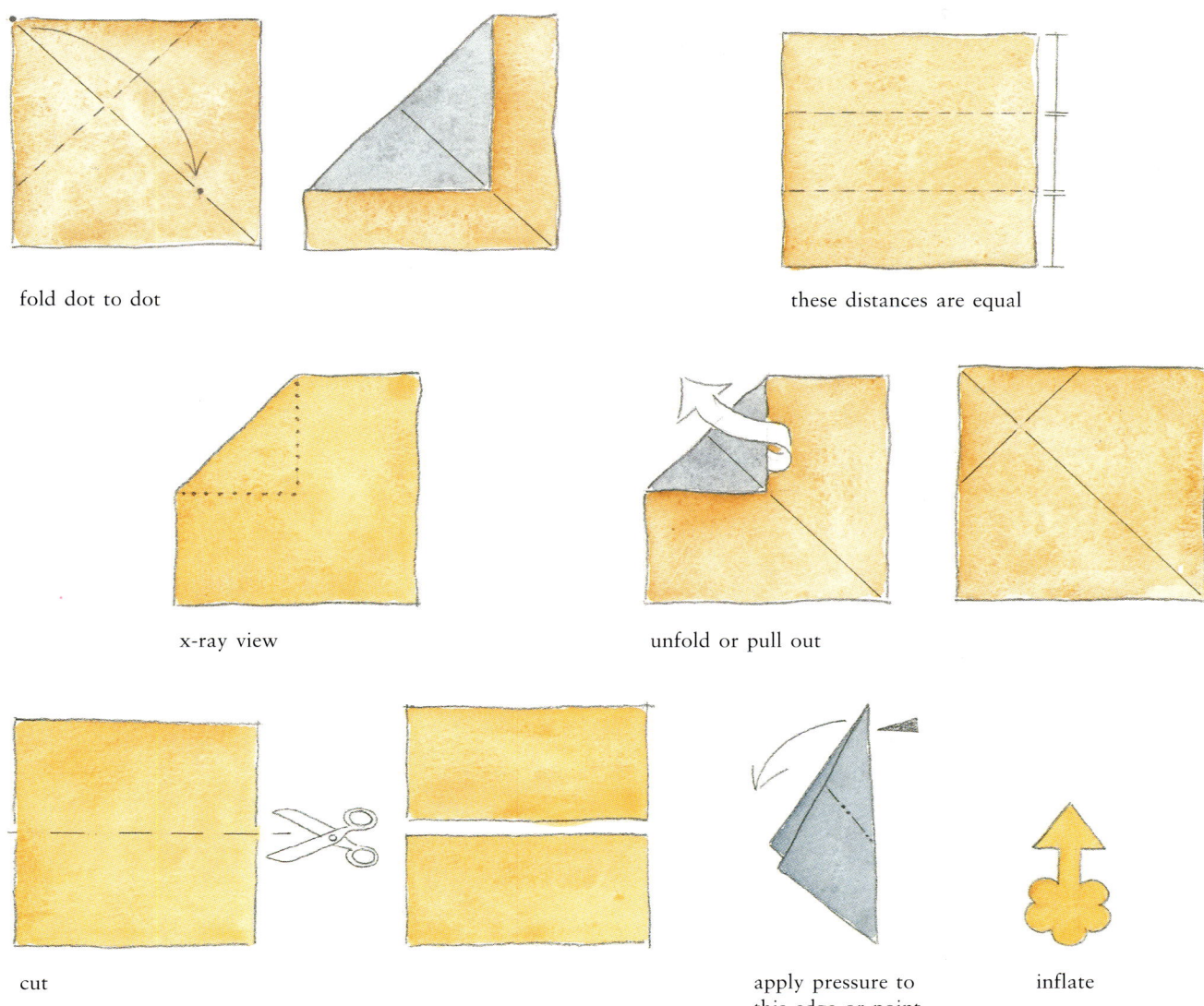

fold dot to dot

these distances are equal

x-ray view

unfold or pull out

cut

apply pressure to
this edge or point

inflate

ADVANCED FOLDING TECHNIQUES

Apart from the basic mountain and valley creases from which all origami designs are folded, there are four advanced techniques found in this book. These techniques are used in combination and are: the squash fold, the sink fold and the inside and outside reverse folds. However, not all designs use these advanced techniques.

Squash and sink folds are the least common. To save space, a detailed explanation of each is given once in the book within a particular design. For an explanation of the squash fold see the Multiform House, Steps 4–6 (page 26); for an explanation of the sink fold see the Star, Steps 8–12 (pages 30–31). When you come across a squash or sink fold in another design, refer to these designs for a step-by-step guide. Inside and outside reverse folds are not more complex than squash or sink folds, but are more common and come in a greater variety.

So, to simplify cross-referencing, here are the basic forms of each. Refer to this page whenever you need to be reminded how to make them.

INSIDE REVERSE

Pull-through version

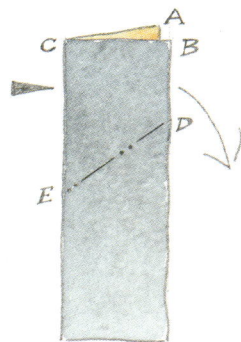

1 This is how the manoeuvre is illustrated in the book.

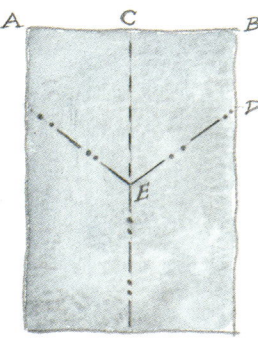

2 This is the crease pattern.

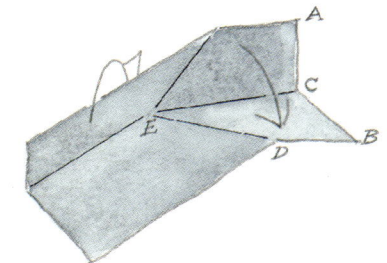

3 Collapse.

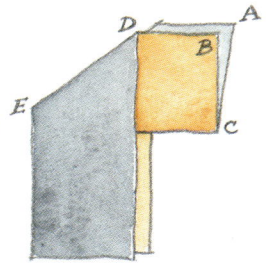

4 Complete.

Push-in version

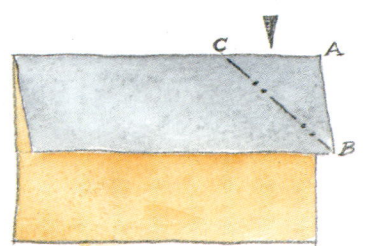

1 This is how the manoeuvre is illustrated in the book.

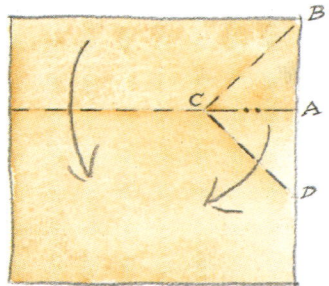

2 This is the crease pattern.

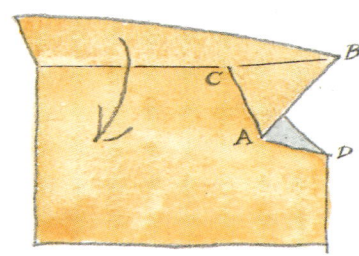

3 Collapse.

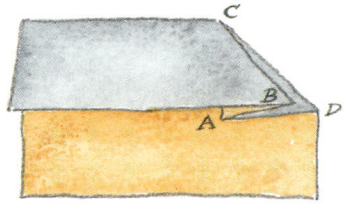

4 Complete.

OUTSIDE REVERSE

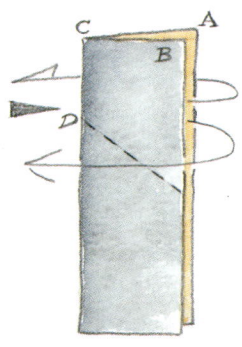

1 This is how the manoeuvre is illustrated in the book.

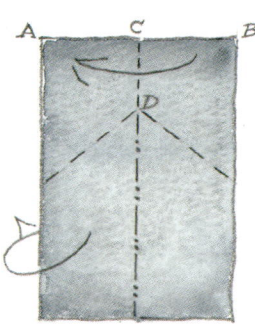

2 This is the crease pattern.

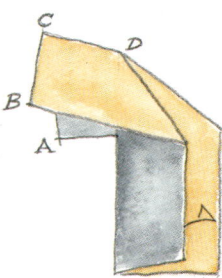

3 Collapse.

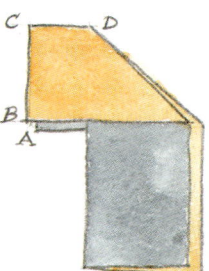

4 Complete.

 # INDEX